Georgia
People and Places

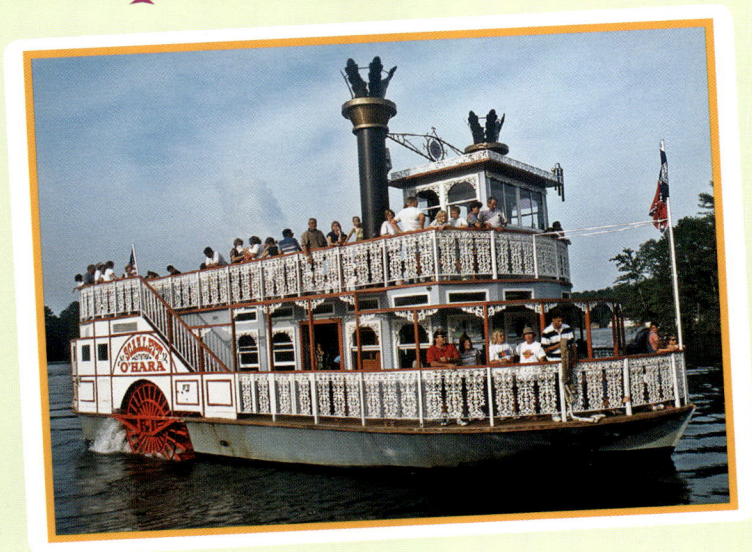

by Tyler Schumacher

Capstone
press
Mankato, Minnesota

Capstone Press
151 Good Counsel Drive, P.O. Box 669, Mankato, Minnesota 56002
www.capstonepress.com

Library of Congress Cataloging-in-Publication Data
Schumacher, Tyler.
 Georgia : people and places / by Tyler Schumacher.
   p. cm.
 Includes bibliographical references and index.
 ISBN-13: 978-0-7368-5826-7 (hardcover)
 ISBN-10: 0-7368-5826-1 (hardcover)
 1. Georgia—Juvenile literature. 2. Georgia—Geography—Juvenile literature. I. Title.
F286.3.S38 2006
975.8—dc22   2005023428

Editorial Credits
Heather Adamson, editor; Linda Clavel, designer; Deirdre Barton, photo researcher

Photo Credits
Betty Crowell, 29; Capstone Press Archives, 28; Capstone Press/Kelly Garvin, 10; Corbis/
Bettmann, 24–25; Corbis/Burstein Collection, 14; Corbis/David Muench, 9, 18–19; Corbis/
Hulton-Deutsch Collection, 25; Corbis/James Randklev, 6; Corbis/Joseph Sohm Inc., 23; Corbis/
Kevin Fleming, 8; Corbis/Royalty Free, 29; Corbis/W. Cody, 26; Corbis/William Manning, cover
(trees with path); Courtesy of Ed Jackson, 20; Daybreak Imagery/Richard Day, 29; Frank H.
McClung Museum, University of Tennessee, Knoxville, 16; Georgia Department of Industry,
Trade & Tourism, cover (cityscape)(canoe)(kids eating peaches), 1, 5, 27; Getty Images Inc., 22;
Henry C. Aldrich, 29; Joel Chandler Harris, 21; Kit Breen, 14–15; Marilyn "Angel" Wynn, 12
(both), 17 (both); North Wind Picture Archives, 11, 13; Stock Montage, Inc., 18

*Capstone Press thanks Linda Renee Gillen from Evoline C. West Elementary, Fulton County, Georgia, for
   her assistance in preparing this book.*

1 2 3 4 5 6 11 10 09 08 07 06

Table of Contents

Something for Everyone

From hip-hop music to farms and parks, Georgia has something for everyone. Mountains, beaches, rivers, and cities fill Georgia's land. More than 8 million people call Georgia home. Georgia's people come from many backgrounds. The land and the people make this state one-of-a-kind.

Georgia Cities

Georgians enjoy the Cherry Blossom Festival in Macon.

Georgia's Land

Hills and fields cover most of Georgia's land. But Georgia has mountains and islands too. With lots of rivers, lakes, and the Atlantic Ocean, Georgia has plenty of water!

The Tallulah River winds through the Chattahoochee National Forest in northern Georgia.

Georgia Land Features

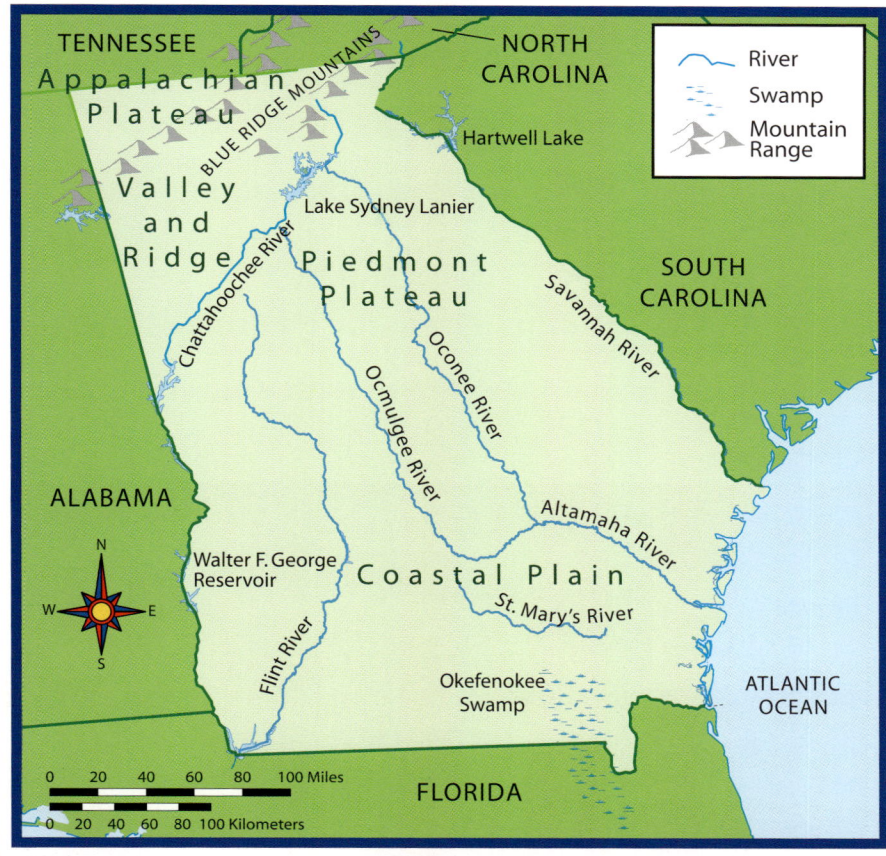

TENNESSEE

Appalachian Plateau

BLUE RIDGE MOUNTAINS

NORTH CAROLINA

Hartwell Lake

Valley and Ridge

Lake Sydney Lanier

Chattahoochee River

Piedmont Plateau

SOUTH CAROLINA

Savannah River

Oconee River

Ocmulgee River

ALABAMA

Altamaha River

Walter F. George Reservoir

Coastal Plain

St. Mary's River

Flint River

Okefenokee Swamp

ATLANTIC OCEAN

FLORIDA

	River
	Swamp
	Mountain Range

0 20 40 60 80 100 Miles

0 20 40 60 80 100 Kilometers

N W E S

The Blue Ridge Mountains and thick forests cover northern Georgia. The large Chattahoochee River begins in the mountains. It flows along Georgia's western border.

The Savannah River rolls along the small slopes of the Piedmont Plateau. It forms the state's eastern border. The Piedmont's flat land makes for great farming. Dams on the rivers provide power and create lakes.

The long Flint River flows from the Piedmont through the Coastal Plain. Farmers use the river to water their crops.

Georgia's Piedmont Plateau and Coastal Plain provide farmland.

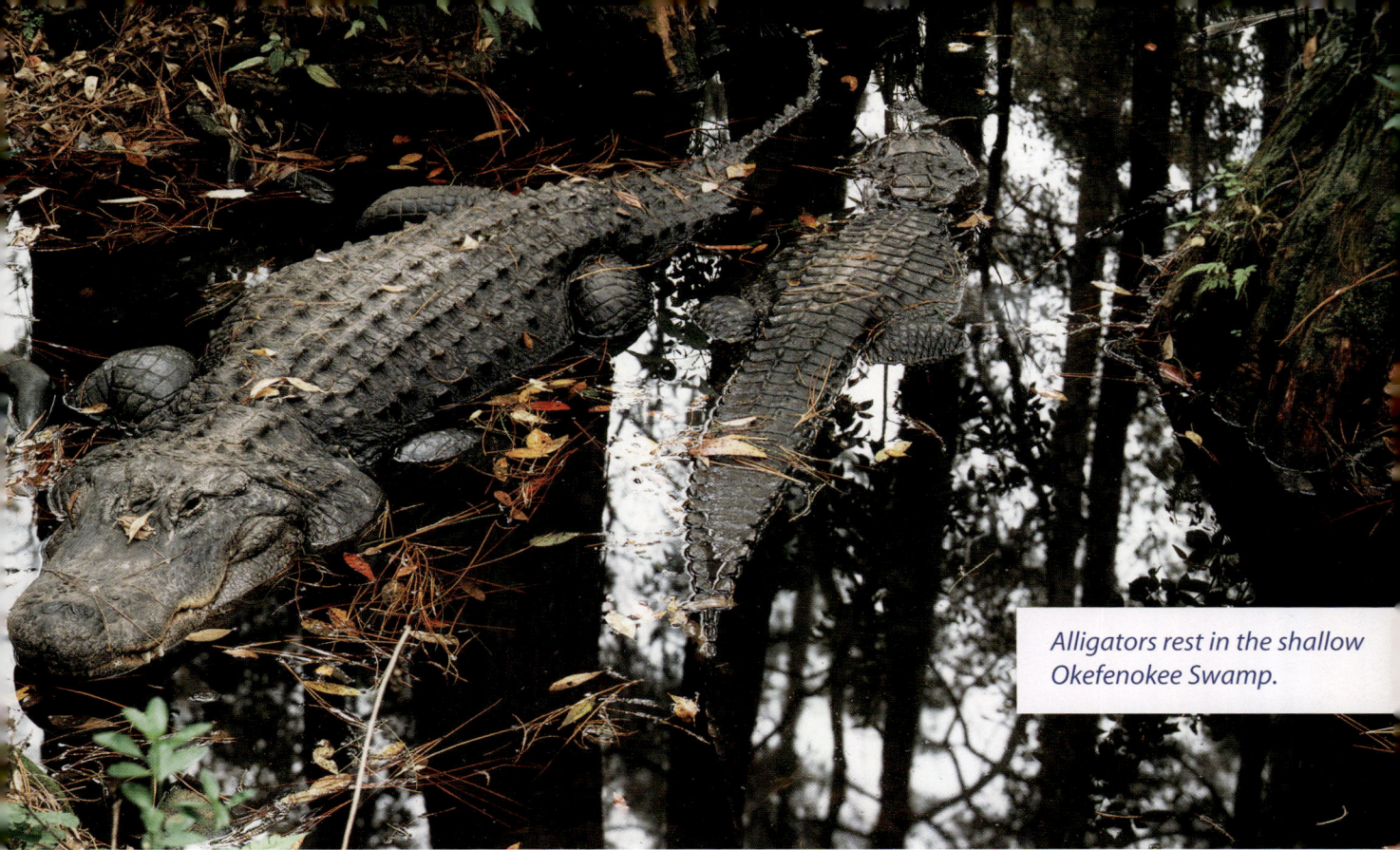

Southern Georgia is home to the Okefenokee Swamp.

Otters, alligators, and birds live among the cypress trees

in this wetland.

A line of islands forms Georgia's southeast edge.

They sit just offshore in the Atlantic Ocean.

The Creek

Green Corn Festival
The Creek started the new year at harvest time. They celebrated with the Green Corn Ceremony. They danced and lit a new fire in the town square. They forgave debts and made new pots. Fresh-picked corn was eaten for the first time that year.

Long ago, Creek Indians built their homes near Georgia's waters. They needed the animals and plants living there for survival. White settlers gave the name Creek to all the American Indians living between the Flint and Chattahoochee rivers.

The Creek used logs and thin branches to build their homes. They spread grass, clay, and mud over the wood to make walls.

Creek towns had an open square for festivals and dancing. They called the square the Pascova.

Creek homes were made from clay and grass. Later, they built log cabins like the white settlers.

The Creek made jewelry from antlers, horns, and bones.

Creek women and children plowed gardens with sticks and animal bones. They planted corn, beans, and squash. They also gathered wild rice and berries.

Creek men hunted deer, turkeys, and rabbits. They used spears and bows and arrows. They also fished. The Creek always shared their food with each other.

The Creek sewed dresses and breechcloths from animal skins and furs. They decorated their clothing with feathers. The Creek also made jewelry from antlers and horns.

In the 1700s, white settlers arrived. The Creek often traded crops and clothing with them. By the 1800s, many Creek dressed like the settlers and built log cabins.

The Creek used animal skins and furs to make their clothes.

13

The Cherokee

Sequoyah's Alphabet

A Cherokee man named Sequoyah saw whites using writing. He wanted the Cherokee to use writing too. In 1821, he invented a writing system called "Talking Leaves." Within a few years almost all the Cherokee could read and write.

Long ago, the Cherokee Indians lived near Georgia's Blue Ridge Mountains. They depended on the land for shelter, food, and clothing.

The Cherokee built dome-shaped homes. They covered branches with sticky mud and clay. Later in the 1800s, the Cherokee built log cabins like white settlers.

Cherokee women tended big squash patches and planted large fields of corn. They gathered wild berries and nuts. The Cherokee snacked on popcorn and cornbread.

Cherokee homes were made from clay and mud. The Cherokee dug the floor down into the ground.

The Cherokee sewed clothing made from Georgia's plants and animals. Women wove plants into skirts. They created deerskin dresses with feather capes. The men wore animal skin leggings and belted robes. The men also decorated their skin with paint and tattoos.

16

Cherokee men hunted bears, deer, and rabbits. They used blowguns and bows and arrows. They made these weapons from cane poles, sticks, and stones. They also speared and netted fish.

Sharpened stones made good arrowheads and spear tips.

The Cherokee used long, hollow blowgun tubes to shoot darts.

Georgia's Beginning

James Oglethorpe
England had crowded prisons in the 1700s. James Oglethorpe believed some prisoners could start a new life in America. Georgia was founded for just these people. Oglethorpe led Georgia's first settlers. He founded the town of Savannah and led the colony during its early years.

Georgia got its name in 1733. English settlers along the Savannah River named the land after their king, George I. The king had sent James Oglethorpe and a group of colonists to this new land.

The colonists worked hard and learned to use Georgia's land. They cleared forests and built log cabins. They planted corn, peas, pumpkins, and squash.

The colonists also had goods shipped from England. Supplies like cloth, guns, and tea helped the colonists feel at home in Georgia.

White settlers cut down trees to build homes. The sturdy log cabins lasted a long time.

James Oglethorpe made a treaty
with Tomochichi for the land
near the Savannah River.

Creek Chief Tomochichi helped the colonists. Tomochichi and Oglethorpe made treaties for land around the Savannah River. The treaties helped the colonists and Indian tribes live peacefully on the same land.

Tomochichi also organized many tribes to trade goods with the colonists. Soon the colonists had all they needed to survive. The town grew to more than 4,000 people by 1753.

As the colony grew, so did the need for more land. White settlers pushed most of the Creek and Cherokee out of Georgia. Some Indians moved west. Most were forced out by the U.S. Army. By the 1840s, very few Indians were left in the state.

Mary Musgrove
Many Georgia treaties could not have been made without Mary Musgrove's help.
Her father was white and her mother was Indian. Musgrove learned to speak both English and Creek languages. She translated for Oglethorpe and Tomochichi.

Georgia's Leaders

Jimmy Carter

Jimmy Carter became one of Georgia's great governors. Leading the state from 1971 to 1975, he passed laws to protect Georgia's rivers. He also worked for all races to be treated equally. Carter is the only Georgian to be elected president of the United States.

Today Georgia's leaders work at the capitol in downtown Atlanta. They meet there to talk about and create new laws.

The governor is the state's highest elected official. Governors lead a state the same way mayors lead cities and towns. They listen to the people and try to make laws to help them.

The dome of Georgia's capitol is covered with gold mined in Georgia.

Jackie Robinson

Until 1947, only whites could play Major League Baseball. A man born in Georgia changed that. Jackie Robinson was the first African American to play in the major leagues. His courage inspired other athletes.

Not all Georgia's leaders are elected. Martin Luther King Jr. was a minister from Atlanta. He wanted different races to get along.

In the 1950s and 1960s, he led marches and rallies. He asked the government to change unfair laws about race. King's work is celebrated as a national holiday.

Martin Luther King Jr. spoke to large crowds like this one in Washington, D.C.

Georgia Today

Today Georgia is a bustling place. Planes roar into and out of Atlanta's airport. Ships cruise into seaports of Savannah and Brunswick. Companies like Coca-Cola and CNN have offices in Georgia skyscrapers.

Skyscrapers in Atlanta are home to many businesses.

Descendants of Creek and Cherokee Indians still live in parts of Georgia. They continue to celebrate festivals like the Green Corn Ceremony. Georgians cheer for pro sports. They watch ballet and opera. They enjoy jazz and bluegrass music performances. Georgia has something for everyone.

Fast Facts

State Flag

State Fruit

Peach

Manufactured Products

Cloth and Clothing, Food and Beverages, Paper

Timeline

Spanish Explorer Hernando de Soto travels through what is now Georgia.

Georgia becomes the fourth state.

Sequoyah invents the Cherokee alphabet.

1540

1733

1788

1820s

1821

1830s

Chief Tomochichi and James Oglethorpe make a treaty allowing the colonists to settle by the Savannah River.

The Creek are forced off their lands and moved west.

The Cherokee are forced off their lands and moved west.

Livestock Products

Chickens, Eggs, Cattle, Hogs

State Flower

Cherokee Rose

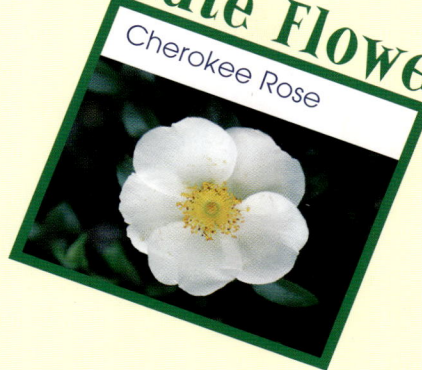

State Bird

Brown Thrasher

State Tree

Live Oak

Farm Products

Cotton, Peanuts, Tobacco, Pecans

Georgia rejoins the United States.

Jimmy Carter serves as president of the United States.

Georgia adopts a new state flag.

1870

1861–1865

1960

1977–1981

1996

2003

Georgia fights as part of the Confederacy during the Civil War.

Martin Luther King Jr. takes part in sit-ins in Atlanta stores.

Atlanta hosts the summer Olympics.

29

Glossary

breechcloth (BREECH-kloth)—a piece of deerskin clothing that hangs from the waist and passes between the legs

colonist (KOL-uh-nist)—a person living in a newly settled area

festival (FESS-tuh-vuhl)—a celebration that is held at the same time each year

found (FOUND)—to set up or start something

piedmont (PEED-mont)—sloping land formed at the foot of a mountain; Georgia's Piedmont Plateau has small hills.

swamp (SWAHMP)—an area of wet, spongy ground

translate (TRANZ-late)—to change words from one language to another

treaty (TREE-tee)—an agreement between two or more groups or countries

Read More

Bograd, Larry. *Uniquely Georgia.* Heinemann State Studies. Chicago: Heinemann, 2004.

Crane, Carol. *P is for Peach: a Georgia Alphabet.* Chelsea, Mich.: Sleeping Bear Press, 2002.

McAuliffe, Emily. *Georgia Facts and Symbols.* The States and Their Symbols. Mankato, Minn.: Capstone Press, 2003.

Internet Sites

FactHound offers a safe, fun way to find Internet sites related to this book. All of the sites on FactHound have been researched by our staff.

Here's how:
1. Visit *www.facthound.com*
2. Type in this special code **0736858261** for age-appropriate sites. Or enter a search word related to this book for a more general search.
3. Click on the **Fetch It** button.

FactHound will fetch the best sites for you!

Index